Elixir

Seeds to Gems

Publisher Information

Published by Mervin Telford

Copyright © 2015 Mervin Telford

Contact the author: elixirpoetry@gmail.com

ISBN: 978-0992954499

Elixir

Seeds to Gems

Mervin Telford

ACKNOWLEDGEMENTS:

TO DENNIS AND EVA KENTON
For their unswerving support, patience in editing and
encouragement.

TO KYRENE BONTERRE
For her professional and efficient editing.

TO ALL OF MY SPIRITUAL MENTORS
I thank you with all my heart for your skill in teaching,
your wisdom, love and fortitude.

THIS WORK IS HUMBLY DEDICATED

TO THE DEVINE FIRST CAUSE.

THANK YOU FOR LIFE, LOVE

AND THE BEAUTY THAT THEY BRING.

IT IS ALSO DEDICATE TO THE MEN

WOMEN AND CHILDREN OF THE

EARTH AND THE UNSEEN

REALMS BEYOND.

MAY THEY HOLD WITHIN THEIR

MINDS AND HEARTS BEAUTIFUL

VISIONS AND LOFTY IDEALS.

THAT THEY WITH A GLAD HEART

WILL ONE DAY REALISE

THIER MOST CHERRISHED DREAMS.

THEN IT WILL BE SAID

"ENTER HERE NOW MY BELOVED".

Elixir

FOREWORD

Welcome, you are about to enter into a world moved by a singular vision of beauty, peace, unity and love. The world within this book is the surprising and transformational world of Elixir. It was inspired by the poet's inner vision of a Utopian dream and encouraged by historical accounts of a once golden age that embellished the peoples of the earth. This book has been created to sooth, rejuvenate and inspire. Elixir will share with you its thought provoking, aesthetic and emotionally pleasing landscape so that you may continue to create more love, togetherness, beauty and understanding in your own inner and outer worlds.

The unique art within Elixir has been designed to uplift, comfort, and often surprise. Positive imagery and symbols are used to compliment many of the poems; they work in unison to convey a message of love within a healing resonance. Feel the vision and enjoy the poems as you travel the geography and experience the deep essences within Elixir.

HISTORICAL ACCOUNTS

The myths of early China passed down through the oral tradition of storytelling, music and poetry tell of an idyllic society within a paradisiacal age. Historian Kwang Tze (*ca.* 400 B.C.) wrote:

"In the age of perfect virtue, they attached no value to wisdom.....
They were upright and correct, without knowing that to do so was righteousness: they loved one another without knowing that to do so was benevolence: they were honest and whole hearted without knowing that it was loyalty; they fulfilled their engagements, without knowing that to do so was good faith; in their simple movements they employed the services of one another, without thinking that they were conferring or receiving any gift. Therefore their actions left no trace, and there was no record of their affairs."

(Myths and legends of China and Japan, pp. 276)

Forward in history, Ovid replays the Latin tradition regarding the golden age as follows:

"The first Millennium was the age of gold:
Then living creatures trusted one another;
People did well without the thought of ill:
Nothing forbidden in the book of laws, no fears, no prohibitions read in bronze, or in the sculpted face of judge and master......

No Brass-lipped trumpets called, nor clanging swords, nor helmets marched the streets. Country and town had never heard of war: and seasons travelled through the years of peace. The innocent earth learned neither spade nor plough: She gave her riches as fruit hangs from tree; grapes dropping from the vine, cherry, strawberry ripened in silver shadows of the mountain, and in the shade of Jove's miraculous tree the falling acorn. Springtime the single season of the year."

(The Metamorphosis, pp. 33-34)

From the *Mahabharata,* the sacred book of Hinduism, comes the following:

"Men neither bought nor sold; there where no poor and no rich; there was no need to labour, because all that men required was obtained by the power of will…..
The Krita Yuga was without disease;
there was no lessening with the years;
there was no hatred, or vanity, or evil thought whatsoever; no sorrow, no fear."

(Indian myth and legend, pp. 107-108)

Now! Let us finally embark on our poetic Journey to Elixir, towards a unique mix of all the former references to a golden age where all are taught and remember the value of service with love. Therefore they remain dynamic, powerfully alive, forever changing and harmoniously evolving.

WELCOME TO ELIXIR
AETAS AUREA

Mervin Telford

THE SCULPTOR

In the beginning was the Void,
And the Void decreed,
"Let there be Intention
And agreement and retention,
Thereby let nothing be destroyed".
And as it was decreed,
So there was fission,
And Intention was deployed.

Intention declared,
"Let there be Imagination and elation,
Let all imagery have relation".
And as it was intended,
So it became.
Thus Imagination came to fame.

Imagination thought,
"Let there be Creation and recreation,
Let all resonant substance
Have its station".
And as it was imagined,
So it appeared.
Thus Creation became revered.

Creation said,
"Let there be geometry
With sound and sight".
And as it was crafted,
So it became.

And then came structure
And melody and light,
And all was pure and resonant and bright.

Soon an image came to Imagination
By Intention,
And was given to Creation
To be allotted its given station.
And Creation gave it form,
Thus was a living sculpture born.

With Intention and Imagination,
Creation agreed to give it breath,
Thereby saving it from death.
And the sculpture was given a name,
It was called "Hu-man, Eternal Flame".
And there historically it stood,
For all to see
That it was good.

Mervin Telford

ZENITH TO A DREAM

The Earth moved in rhythm
With the Universe's pounding heart.
Star lights flickered,
Danced like fireflies in her heavens.
Then!
Suddenly, all forms became nebulous.
Solids became fluid and vague
But waters turned rigid
Like glaziers of glass.
Then all things collapsed.
Folding in on themselves.
Changing before startled senses.
In an instant
Humanity faced itself.
Its joint mind aflame with
The words "What is happening?"
A new global requiem.
Reverberating mantra of repair.
Billions of former selves now
Welcomed into a new realm.
Known by this transformer,
Giver of new light,
Bestower of eternal gifts.
All have entered into a
Mode of readjustment.
There were no countries, borders,
Rich and poor for those who
Chose to continue and
Take the journey forward.

They, then strengthened by the sieve
Of self re-examination, reclaimed the
Key to the heart, mind and soul
And made the crossing to Elixir,
Zenith to a dream.

Mervin Telford

INTO THE STREAMS

How far will we go this time?

Remembrance,

Love,

Into the stream of water.

Remembrance,

Love,

Into the streams of light.

I will again embrace you.

I will say "yes" and live.

You touch my heart and smile.

"Yes,

We understand "

See the joys of all beings revealed.

Mervin Telford

RE IGNITED

"Awake, awake,

We sleep no more.

Retrieved the torch

Long laid to store.

The mind has served

To fit the parts.

The torch ignites

With faith filled hearts."

A flame again

It lights the way

And rainbow playgrounds

It does display.

Mervin Telford

A NEW PLANE, "ELIXIR"
A NEW NAME.

We came,
We saw,
We planted.
We grew,
We continually nourished her,
We mindfully fed.
We looked on
In believe, awe and wonder;
At this healthy, bountiful spread.

We honeyed her breath
With sweet fragrances.
Building a wholesome,
Vibrant atmosphere,
We continued with our plans
With the utmost respect and care.

We replenished with new forests,
Enriching the soil beneath.
We created energy pyramids,
Health, joy and life to
Our children we bequeath.

We imbued with natural beauty,
We made this a haven of wealth,
We returned deserts to
Wondrous tropical jungles.

Then ran programs,
Providing nutrients'
Improving our health.

We filled her veins with
Medicinal balm,
Arteries increased their flow.
Yearly expanding waters up river = plenty.
All were grateful,
We wanted it to show.

We! manifested our glorious dreams,
Enjoyed our new found gains.
Worked with our various talents,
Supporting our common aims.
Intelligently and intuitively
Continuing to become true and strong.
We travel with laughter and banter,
Work in rapture and song.

Now she shines in splendour.
We gratefully give to adorn.
By truth, peace and empowerment,
From her emerging splendour
We have all been re-born.

Mervin Telford

SERUM OF CHANGE

Penetrating light.
Bright atoms into
Silken tissues sink.
Cellular change,
Exact and exciting.
A tonic
To enhance how we think.
In freedoms engine
Burns a vascular fire.
Joint mindsets
Embraced in a blink.
These stages sent to bless us.
Positive imagery
Our minds gently drink.

What fuels us to gather
Our essence?
Love! the energy of life
Attached to blood.
Consciously gifting the
Dreams of the dreamer.
As glorious smiles pour
Down from above.
Intuitively gifted.
These beautiful feelings.
They serve to
Strengthen our stance.
All are attuned and attentive;
To our souls' ascending dance.

The sound of silence,
White light is revealing.
The poets' pen, it
Writes again, and again.
Visions are born and created.
Spirit developed
And elected to reign.
New Jewels are uncovered.
Mined with care
For us to arrange.
Love has propelled
This age-old prediction.
This metamorphic
Serum of change.

Mervin Telford

BORN

Gasp!

Broken waters are flowing.

A new face

Into comfort is born.

Fired into bright light,

Innocence staring.

Gift wrapped

In a tiny form.

A mother's,

Father's prayers,

Gently unfolded.

Tears with smiles on,

Flower petals and curly lips.

Heartfelt

Warm congratulations.

From time's fountain

Youth is gently eclipsed.

PEACE AND LOVE

"Peace and Love"
Many suns ago we
Welcomed you ashore
With bright lights blazing
From your gaze.
You embraced us,
"United us as one people".
We believed in you,
Nurtured you,
Fed and clothed you with
Humility, faith and trust.
You came to us
And now we are one.
You are our conscience,
Strength, knowledge and
The light of our Sun.

"Peace and love"
With your lessons and laughter
You have seen us grow
Upright, tall and strong.
Patiently you watched the
Colour filled skies with us,
Guided us with great vision,
A new name,
A language filled with joy.
In answer to our prayers
You came bearing great gifts.

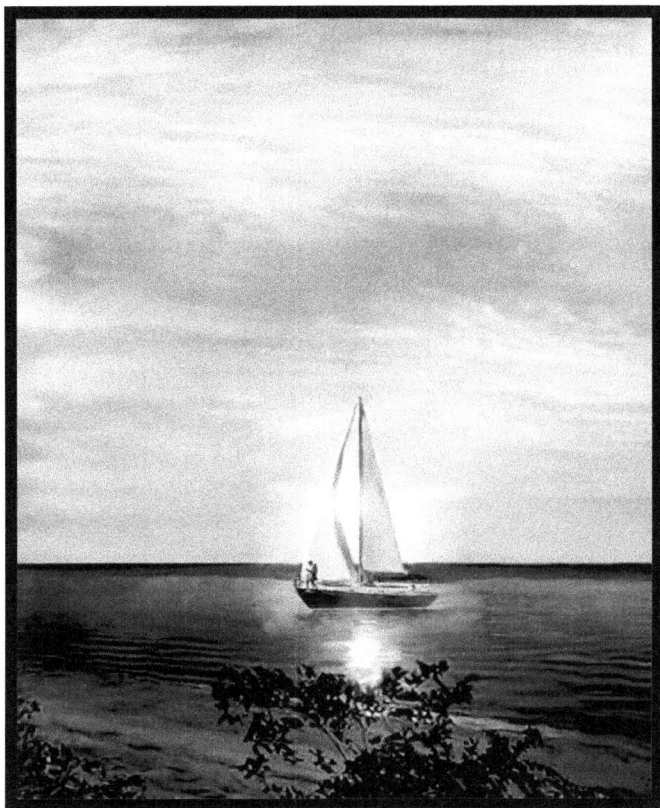

Mervin Telford

We are in love with life.
With you our hearts
Have made a bond.
We are alive to smile and laugh
Rejoicing as one with you.

BY THE WATER'S EDGE

Our dreams are like pearls,

Reclaimed and laid to shore

Delivered by a mighty sea.

When we walk by the water's edge

And see our precious dreams

We give them their breath of life once more.

When we see them naked,

Glistening in the midday sun

We call out with our thoughts

And all come to gather, clothe

And nurture them as one.

When we walk by the water's edge

And see our precious dreams

We give them their breath of life once more.

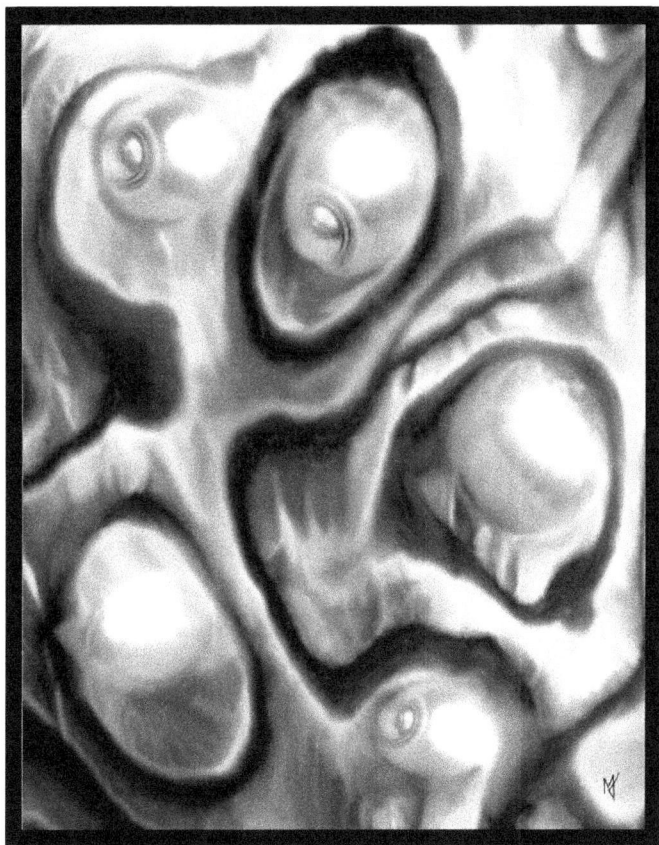

Mervin Telford

SOJOURNERS

We accept what is given and rise.

We rise,

Travelling the heroes' path.

Into the heights.

High into the mystery,

Unfolding journeys into bliss.

Rivers of the heart and mind.

This,

Only this for us is real.

Mervin Telford

SECOND BREATH

The tapestry's needle is
Threaded with care,
In answer to life's longing
And her indefinite prayer.
Distant voices,
Audible bubbling,
Refined fluids that flow;
I am the arrow
That waits to be sent by the bow.

Liquid enriched,
Resting,
Born, yet unborn,
Happily dreaming,
I move my tiny form.
Nurturing care,
Soothing waves of
Concern from above,
How close the voice
That speaks of sweet solace and love.

Echoes travel my chamber
As I move gently around,
Sweet voices,
Nature's chants,
Musical melodies sound.
When all is silent,
Two audible harmonies
Pulsate as one;

They reassure me,
My tapestry's course will be run.

Focused,
Calm,
Heart pulsing,
Umbilicaly fed.
Soft energies move bones and
Preparatory thoughts in my head.
Relaxing sensations,
Eased from head to toe,
Released into brightness,
I'm sent forth by the bow.

Breath of life
Light assisted,
They said "Breathe": I obeyed!
Caressed,
Washed,
Dried,
And gently allayed.
Friendly noises surround me,
My smiling family stand and stare.
My matriarch receives me
And feeds me with care.

THE GOOD NEWS

Sshshh, do you see it?
Something is very special!
And within sight.
We, Elixir's children
With lighter hearts
Have seen truths freed
And in full flight.
Propagating humility,
Courage agendas
And new life speeches.
Re-told and bright.
Awakened energies
And life affirmations
Securing inner warmth.
New built bridges
Give rise to more answers.
The master dispenser
Teaches to love
All who are sent.
A noble road!
Who are they?
What do they look like?
We say, "all who can hear,
See or touch, of any
Shape, age or colour",
The master's code,
Lived with intent.

Mervin Telford

And who is most masterful?
"The I am all"
And the word has spread,
Ask the hallowed being.
The people are joyous.
Mass awakened.
Security restored and
Global empathy is now enjoyed,
And all artists are employed.
"Freedom of speech is abundant".
Truth enjoyed means
The colour on the brush is
Deployed and vibrant.
Painting exhilarating scenes
On canvases,
Gloriously arrayed and recumbent.

People growing in the winds,
Like ascending trees.
While gardeners feed the planet
And everyone believes.

Sshshh, quiet,
Do you hear it?
Something sounds beautiful,
Exchanged,
Changed.
Our people are with song.
Exuding and growing.
Immunity strengthened.
DNA re-arranged
Self governing,
Self realising,
Showing
Soothing new riches.
Elixir's children are re-born,
Healing,
Glad hearts yielding
Faces smiling.
The good news
Taught with truth and feeling.
We are harvesting new crops,
And are giving freely.

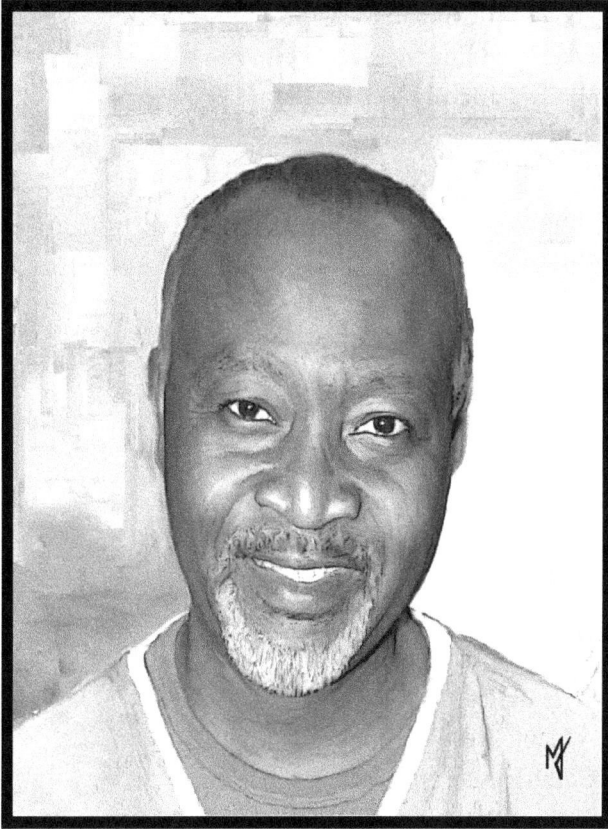

Mervin Telford

A mighty yield means no more buying.
Faces are radiant and bodies
Leaner, faster and stronger,
Giving and with love, applying
The warming fruits of
The great harvest supplying
Plentiful.
My people with joy are crying.

People, growing in the winds
Like ascending trees.
While gardeners feed the planet
And everyone believes.

Shhhshh, quiet.
Do you smell it?
Breathe,
Something is sweet!
Warm and fragrant,
Senses made keen,
The fragrant ground walked on
With perfumed new feet.
Togetherness, peace,
And understanding,
Wisdom expanding!
Room for thought and cause
Serendipity,
A blank sheet,
Children safe and playing.

Wolves watching lovingly
With lambs playing.
Organic and with comfort
New clothes
For new souls
Bringing unity and live manifestos,
United agenda
Utilitarianism magnifying.
A healed planet,
Yielding healing balms
To an excelling, healthy people.
Wholesome ecologies

Mervin Telford

With the new oracles.
Love,
Knowledge,
Aesthetics,
And unity games
Means
Fully cognisant young
With internal dreams,
Externally projected,
Mental premonitions,
Utopian prophecies realised.
The wise man walks
And talks again.

People, growing in the winds
Like ascending trees.
While gardeners feed the planet
And everyone believes.

Shhshh, do you feel it?
Something very special.
We are harvesting with
Celebration
Seeds, nuts, grains and
Exotic fruits
And vegetables shining,
Colourful and alive.
Dancing with visible riches.
Utopia,
Land of milk and honey.

Mervin Telford

Released formula,
Tried and tested.
Natural and work invested.
People are creating and happy
With the golden wings of freedom.
Drinking a new Elixir.
A relish and a wonder.
An ode to honesty.
The time-delayed dream.
The light,
The night
And the peaceful slumber
In the heart of the dream weaver.
Inhaling, exhaling magnetised love.
Giving gifts like falling stars
And every store is an open
Energy giver
To replenish evermore
The joint river of the heart and mind.
The present is loaded
We have remembered
It is the collective that helps us deliver.

People, growing in the winds
Like ascending trees.
While gardeners feed the planet
And everyone believes.

THROUGH CAT'S EYES

Fluorescent flora
Parts gracefully against our heads.
We arch our backs and limber up.
Jaws stretching with
Sounding yawns and muted roars.
Awaiting further exploration are
The beautiful and fragrant Elixian fields.
This plentiful region is home.
Here we are nourished and revived
And all who arrive here are as family.

Plumes of clouds drift gracefully overhead
Adding movement to the orange Sun.
As with all days,
This day is silken and warm.
Momentarily we see other eyes.
Beaming with life,
Silent and appreciative
In common communion
And thanksgiving.

Vegetables, fruits, nuts and grains,
All lay and hang thick and ripe
In the colour filled landscape.
Our cubs run and play freely with
Elixian children. Gentle hands and paws,
Glistening teeth, angled smiles and soft purrs.
Their eager minds play and explore
And we behold them with much love.

Mervin Telford

With golden velvet coats,
Our movement is keen
On this rich, brilliant day
We feed and are fed
And welcome all who join us.

BEACON

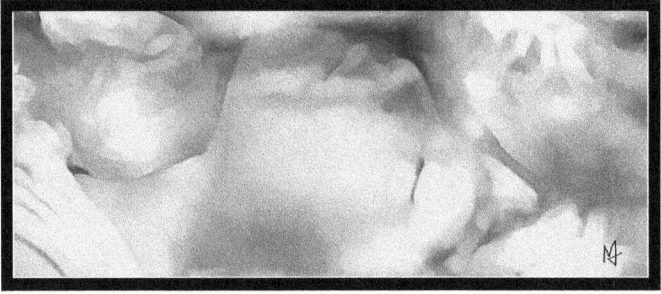

Mervin Telford

In cotton landscapes
Dreams a child,
In ethereal slumber
Held so mild.
It sees the light
In an awakened state,
Guided by a torch gifted
By guardians great.
From triangular pillars
The torch lights the way
And rainbow playgrounds
It does display.

Under sunlit skies
The child awoke,
Took the torch
Abroad with hope.
"To see its inner parts!"
It spoke,

"To show its works
I will surprise,
To reveal its heart
To sibling's eyes."

Mervin Telford

A teacher now
From sapling grown.
The being became
A Tree well known.
The torches light
Shines from their core.
The sibling's havens
Have been restored.
Love surrounds
The being this day,
Shared the gift
That lit the way.

GIFTS FOR YOUR JOURNEY

As expected you left.
We smiled and sent our love
To further nourished you
On your journey.
Through our kinship
We built bridges
Made of laughter,
Understanding and empathy;
They will stand throughout time.
In our minds we still see your face
Sometimes through a haze
Of joy filled tears.

As the years pass
We cherish your invisible energy
That is felt even from afar.
We sing in remembrance of your
Healing, your love and wisdom.
Your words of assurance echo
Within the universe of our minds
And resonate delicately in
The robust chambers of our hearts.

You have gone
Yet you are still with us.
Our fabric was born from
Your words,
Your mind,
Your heart and soul.

We honour you,
Continuing your legacy of
Awakening and transformation
We are forevermore
Your loving siblings.

Mervin Telford

LOVE TO BE WORN

LOVE TO BE WORN
LOVE WEAVE

Love			Love			Love		
Suits you			suits you			suits you		

You should wear it more often. You should wear it more often. You should wear it more often

Out in the open			out in the open			out in the open		
As a token			As a token			As a token		
Of good			Of good			Of good		
Will	Love	Love	Will	Love	Love	Will		
It	I love you I love you		It	I love you I love you		It		
Is	I love you I love you		Is	I love you I love you		Is		
A	I love you I love		A	I love you I love		A		
Joy	You love I		Joy	You love I		Joy		
To see	I love		To see	I love		To see		
Smiles because	I		Smiles because	I		Smiles because		

Love really suits you. Love really suits you Love really suits you

You should wear it more often. You should wear it more often. You should wear it more often

Out in the open,			Out in the open			Out in the open		
As a token			As a token			As a token		
Of good			Of good			of good		
Will	Love	Love	will	Love	Love	will		
It	I love you I love you		It	I love you I love you		It		
Is	I love you I love you		Is	I love you I love you		Is		
A	I love you I love		A	I love you I love		A		
Joy	You love I		Joy	You love I		Joy		
To see	I love		To see	I love		To see		
Happiness as	I		Happiness as	I		Happiness as		

Love really suits you Love really suits you Love really suits you

You should wear it more often. You should wear it more often. You should wear it more often

Out in the open			Out in the open			Out in the open		
As a token			As a token			As a token		
Of good			Of good			Of good		
Will	Love	Love	Will	Love	Love	Will		
It	I love you I love you		It	I love you I love you		It		
Is	I love you I love you		Is	I love you I love you		Is		
A	I love you I love		A	I love you I love		A		
Joy	You love I		Joy	You love I		Joy		
To see	I love		To see	I love		To see		
Laughter as	I		Laughter as	I		Laughter as		

Love really suits you Love really suits you Love really suits you

You should wear it more often. You should wear it more often. You should wear it more often

Out in the open			Out in the open			Out in the open		
As a token			As a token			As a token		
Of good			Of good			Of good		
Will	love	Love	Will	love	Love	Will		
It	I love you I love you		It	I love you I love you		It		
Is	I love you I love you		Is	I love you I love you		Is		
A	I love you I love		A	I love you I love		A		
Joy	You Love I		Joy	You Love I		Joy		
To feel	I love		To feel	I love		To feel		
loved as	I		Loved as	I		Loved as		

Love really suits you Love really suits you Love really suits you

You should wear it more often. You should wear it more often. You should wear it more often.

Love
Suits you
You should wear it more often.
Out in the open
As a token

Of good

Will

It

Is

A

Joy

To see

Smiles because

Love really suits you.

You should wear it more often.

Out in the open,

As a token

Of good

Will

It

Is

A

Joy

To see

Happiness as

Love really suits you

You should wear it more often.

Out in the open

As a token

Of good

Will

It

Is

A

Joy

To see

Laughter as
Love really suits you
You should wear it more often.
Out in the open
As a token
Of good
Will
It
Is
A
Joy
To feel
Loved as
Love really suits you
You should wear it more often.

Love   Love
I love you I love you
I love you I love you
I love you I love
You love I
I love
I

ALIVE

Great Spirit Devine,

We are with you now

As you dream,

Weaving together

The lives of the named,

Married to an infinite journey.

We glory in your love

As we forever remember this,

Our matrimonial bond,

Here with you,

We are alive,

Alive forever with you.

LOVE DANCE

Like the soft light of a new dawn
Breaking over a field of Elixian spices,
You are fragrant.
Charged with subtle flowing energies,
You are like heavenly children,
Joyfully playing in colour filled winds
To melodies not yet heard by mortal ears.

You are like sublime notes,
Played by ethereal instruments,
Caught in the ever-changing current of life.
Holding you is like dancing with an angel,
Like touching the wind,
Like gently caressing silk
With a feather light touch.

You are spiritual strength and beauty
Born of joy in life and love.
You are the healer who comes to be healed,
The giver who comes to receive.
You are born to be loved,
Are caught in a beam of love,
And therefore emanate love effortlessly.
You are a lifetime of silent prayers
Answered in an exquisite waking dream.

Mervin Telford

You are the sun
That brings the seed to bear its golden fruit.
You are all these things and much more.
To know you is to truly cherish the moment
And now time will be a friend to our love.

THE PLEDGE

Mervin Telford

Joy,
Elation,
Flowering creation,
Love rises,

Ignited,
Serenity released.
It graces the air,
Floats in on elation,
Embracing with freedom,
It's divinity's high priest

He stands smiling,
Heart tender with age.
She stands rejoicing,
On her beautiful stage.
Their words are building,
Growing,
It's a wonderful display.
They pledge
Love eternally,
Verbally caressed,
Trembling,
Exhilarated this day.

His eyes warm
And tender
Jubilant
The family rejoice,
She shivers, blissfully
Beholding her choice.
Warm embrace,
His loving arms surround.
Their true love glows
And Shines all around

Mothers with tears of joy.
A family is blissful today.
Faith has released its harvest
A wonderful display.
Pledges heard with feeling.
Joy and laughter abounds.
Food, enlivening Music,
Dancing and rhythmic sounds.
All come to celebrate
The pledge of respect.
This resplendent union
Their love will reflect.

TEACHERS

Akashic recordings

Are explained from their oceans.

Students rise to the prayers

Spoken from their tongue.

A symphony resonating

To the tempo of the soul's desires.

Encouragement

For the mature and the young.

Unfolding gifts

Are exuded in their presence.

Abroad and travelling,

Greeting the class that has come.

Strong limbed

And strengthening the hearts

Of the receptive.

A vocation so delicately spun.

New taught souls

Walk with healing and vigour.

Emblazoned are the

Chambers of the heart.

Encouraging with love and devotion.

As classes ascend

The teachers survey the

Beautiful yield of their art.

GOLDEN CHALICE

Gentle heart,

Golden chalice

My soul mate.

Warm words

Genuine soul

Dreams merged.

Entwined energy

Inner knowing

I love you.

Importance growing

Common cause

Souls converged.

Mervin Telford

GRATITIUDE

Great Spirit Father, Mother,

Ether, Fire, Wind, Water, Earth.

We thank you

As you love and spread your arms.

In your gentle, warm embrace

You guide and strengthen us

To live in harmony

And we embrace your natural balms.

Mervin Telford

AN ODE TO LOVE

Love is elation aimed

Radiating to pulse of life.

Love is the heart

Gone awry with liberation

Made from the gain of

Joyous self allied.

Love is a fresh meadow basking

In the light of its own making.

It is giving only to receive

That which is born by empathy

And grateful tear alike.

Love is ever evolving to the

Prompt of the inner ear

And inner eye.

Love is eternally weighed and

Measured by the unlimited

Scope of the heart.

Love is a suit bestowed

By the grand tailor,

Made to fit the light of the

Wearer whose light shines

Brightest in the eyes

Of their beloved.

Love is internal wishes heard

Aloud by creation

And strives only to serve,

Especially those who believe

In its offering.

Like destiny,

Love rises from ashes

Into flame again and again.

It impassions the sincere to

Seek their reflection in

The eyes of their betrothed,

Longing for themselves to

Be enveloped as one.

Love is a being embellished

With healing hands.

Is the souls' pounding hooves

Heard then silenced as it finds

The air with ethereal wings unbound.

Love speaks through tips of

Silken lips that find passion

In that moment of fire,

That flame that bursts forth

From the furnace of life's

Yearning to be absorbed,

A volcanic vortex

Spiralling towards repose.

Love binds us,

Yet it sets us apart,

For its length, breadth and

Wisdom is far beyond us,

Even as it is part of us.

This is love.

PROPHET

Joyfully I have returned and
Proudly I behold you with awe.
You have planted the best of
Yourselves in your gardens.
You grow, strengthen and flourish.
Nourishing all the good that is there.

Long ago after my departure,
You cast fond memories of me
Into sunlit southern winds.
Exhilarated,
I grew, rose and flew.
Bringing warmth to your dreams.

While I travelled;
You gathered and sang loving
Songs from your hearts.
I recognised your souls' melodies
And attributed a clear voice
To each one of you.

You have embellished my
Journey with love
And sweet fragrances.
You have helped to guide my senses
As I helped prepare this,
And many other of your golden havens.

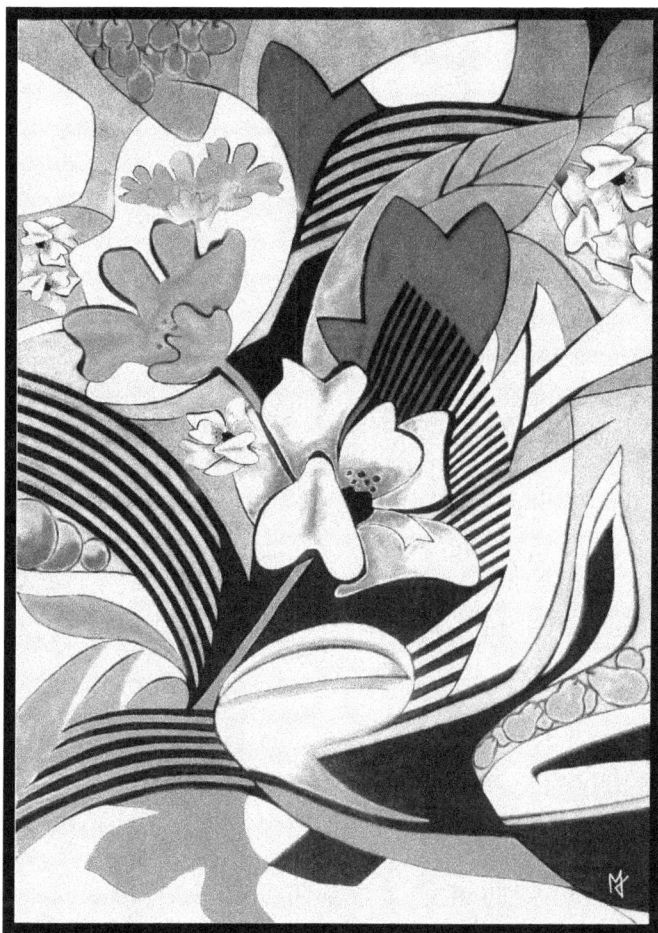

Mervin Telford and Eva Kenton

EUPHORIA'S POEM

Come near to me.
Invoked by words
That convey love.
Sweet song of birds.

Worn halo bright.
Impassioned will.
Emotions soothed.
And calmed with skill.

Nurtured vessel
Light and strong.
Come close sweet love
For we belong.

Maintain our power
In mind and will.
Mantle of courage.
Essence still.

Euphoria's elixir
Has come to distil.
By pouring out love
The Divines' great will.

To create for all
Is the hearts delight.
Feathers caressed
In Spiritual flight.

Eternally magnified
Focused intent
Manifested as paradise
This great ascent.

Mervin Telford

THE ART PARTY

Paintings and sculptures
Sing and convey
On display
Creative signatures
Open inner doors
Re – creating with a personal touch,
Cerebrally caressing,
Mind merging with every line,
Curve, gradient of light.
Reaching out to
Surface and crevice.
An inter-dimensional holiday,
Dining from a menu of
Exquisite melodious hues
And subtle orchestral aesthetics.
We are ecstatically satiated.
I call this a true art party.

Architecture?
Bricks, Wood,
Steel beams,
Panels, nails and rails.
Concrete, glass,
In Stone? NO! Not here.
This is organic, sentient matter.
Self sufficient, self regulating
And owner integrated.
With glassless
Energy shield windows;

Geometric and self organised.
Opaque and soothing with dancing curves
Within photo chromatic skin relays and ethereal
lighting.
Space saving, functional spirals;
Designed with love and care.
Inviting the onlooker to imagining themselves as
The contemporary occupant.
(Colour scheme personality integrated.)

"Hi, are you enjoying the party?"
I exhale,
"Now this I call a progressive, fantastic art party!"

Accompanying musicians
Play Instruments
That speak with colour.
Sublime atoms vibrate.
Ricocheting filaments.
Finely dotted currents,
Streaming from one
Surface to another.
A visual, auditory display.
Like a Rembrandt and Picasso
Mixed, transformed
And with Mozart sent to air.
Every note visually born,
Iridescent and magically seen.
This is sublime music
Mixed with art,
Viewed with awe at this
Amazing art party.

WISDOM COMES QUIETLY

Wisdom comes quietly,

In silence it unfolds,

Guiding the fires of the mind.

From success it leaves bookmarks,

So we can read and re-read and

Help others to leave their bookmarks.

In knowing love it gives a promise

To the children of tomorrow.

Its feathered wings

Bear the lightened load,

And when we surrender

To the majesty of time,

Wisdom comes beautifully

And quietly.

Mervin Telford

TOGETHER

Sweet mothers,
Daughters comb their hair.
Wives set song to sail.
A smile,
A gift to the day embraced,
Children's fathers recount a tale.

In heavenly citadels
Guardians sit,
Emit peace,
A glorious glow.
Fly circling from shining spires
To ensure love's gentle flow.

With equal passion
They love with might.
Teach to heal by will.
Masters and heroes
Loved by us
We glory in their skill.

Exhilarant joy,
Warm endless bliss.
Elite creators serve.
Divine resonances
Received by us.
Gifts for all deserved.

WE PRAY

Prayer rises,
Swelling from focused passion.
Through our hearts and minds we create
By giving thanks with love for all that
We have, then reverently requesting
Continued balance, joy and love for our
Great family.
Intently, Divinity listens
And divinely continues to offer.

We perceive even the subtlest of gifts
And humbly choose to gratefully
Receive our bounteous treasures.
By our thoughts, words and actions
The Devine has been more than gracious
And true in listening and offering.
In prayer we are grateful and conscious in
Our thanksgiving and ever mindful in
Which manner we ask.

GUARDIANS

You are silent,
Meek,
Yet strong.
Receiving tempered flames
That tri-radiate
From our central sun
That reigns.

We are transformed to youth,
By you we are honoured,
Entranced by truth.
The "I am all" is wise,
He made you
Transistor
Healers of surprise.

In your presence
All remain sane.
Nature and the elements
United,
Bounteous again and gain.
Dynamics are turned to balm
By your grace and loving charm.

Ancient energies gently reside
Respectfully by your side.
Covered in beam of light,
Warm light shining bright.

In you we see
The guardian's key.
For as you grow true and free,
We are healed and see.

Mervin Telford

LIKE SUNRISE

Your light touches me now.

To life ẙou say a prayer

That radiates in sweet silence.

Your heightened senses

Alert, receptive and free.

The warmth of your smile and

Embrace, they surprise,

They always surprise.

My love echoes

Into the soul of you,

Into the heart of you,

Into the essence of your gaze

And we rise,

Together we rise.

Mervin Telford

TANGERINE SKIES

Hippopotamus heads
Are floating,
Dark islands.
A large silhouette stands
With siphoning trunk.
The mammoths descendent is swaying
While Elixir's waters are gently drunk.

Sunlit skies,
Strawberry streaks,
Reds merge into oranges.
Tangerine clouds
Pierced with horizontal yellow hues.
The jaguar's retinol receptors are
Dining on a feast of spectacular dusk views.

Mervin Telford

On the horizon
The disc of fire is slowly sinking.
Glowing,
Orange-yellow,
Giant ball of the sun.
Sharp palms cast lazy long shadows
As insects play symphonies,
Nocturnal melodies have begun.

Fragrance inhaled,
Rich and moist,
Tropical sunset.
Visually breathed in with easy eyes.
The boats hull slides
By croaking frogs
Through trickling waters.
Breeze-caressed faces
Are dazzled by tangerine skies.

Mervin Telford

BAKERS' SACRAMENT

Mervin Telford

This mix is kneaded
With delicate skill,
As vibrant souls glide
The beckoning will.
Inner ease caresses,
Causing the heart to bestow,

Energies are forming
A radiant dough.

Shining bright
From head and jaw,
Words trickling
Bright powder,
Knowledge rising
Ever more.
The magic of truth?
The baker's sieve,
Inner prayer,
True friends arrayed,
With pure bread to share.

Dispensing
Nourishment,
Giving food:
We are fed.
Souls receptive,
Baking
Sacramental bread.
Watered and nurtured
In magnificent bloom,
Students with smiles on,
In the Bakers' school room.

Supple minds looking forward,
Expectant and keen.
Loaves rising,
The suns fire,
A heart warming scene.

Aromatic and shimmering,
All in good time.
Our bakers take materials
And makes them sublime.
The permeating essence,
Fragrant, heady and fine.
The loaves' are all connected,
Their offerings refined.

Birthed are our dreams,
Friends are in full flight.
A luminous halo
Is drawn near
By our light.
Magic and ecstatic,
Hearts floating and minds free,
This permeating beauty,
A visual melody.
In sun light you'll see us,
The bakers sacrament we
Embrace.
The Grand baker ever watching
And smiling with grace

YOU LOVE ME

You are iridescent sovereign,
I am royal hue.
You are Mother, Father,
I am body, sky and stars.
You are the infinite garden.
In you I dream and grow
And you love me.

You are the eternal breath,
I am spirit exhaled.
You are purest essence,
And I the ascending message.
You are the unfathomable Playwright,
I embellish with laughter and tears,
And you love me.

You are the life giving sun
And I the dancing fire.
You are the nurturing heart,
I am the warm cradle.
You are the word divine,
Through speech I bear your children
And you love me.

You are the turquoise seas
And I the merciful soil.
You are infinite beginning,
I am the ongoing end.
You are the colour filled horizon
Within which I am gently embraced,
And you will always love me.

MAHOGANY CRADLE

Mahogany cradle,
Soft nest of love.
I lay in comfort,
Graceful smiles from above.

Mahogany cradle,
Under crystalline eyes.
Through silk-filled clouds
My spirit flies.

Mervin Telford

Mahogany cradle,
Fragrant, gentle and deep.
Warm and surrounded,
Awakened from sleep.

Mahogany cradle,
Under stratum skies.
Nurtured by sunlight,
Forever tender surprise.

Mervin Telford

TEMPLE OF LOVE

My parents' world is
Beautifully harmonic.
Meaningful words
Spoken with a sensitive view.
Peace has entered its bookmarks,
Aesthetically pleasing
And well within view.
Comfort and care is radiant.
Our Spirits delicately fed.
Our thirst gently
Quenched by our guardians.
The angelic prevail overhead.

The need to give love,
Care and affection.
The memory of a helping hand.
Alleviating with food,
Care and shelter.
Feeding the gardens
That a loving God planed.
The reminiscent overture.
Angels shine light all around.
A heavenly requiem surrounds us.
Princes and princesses
Victoriously crowned.
As children we are happy
And playing.
Guardians attentive and kind.

Healing balms,
A hand offered in friendship.
Humbled, we are
Watered and dined.
Spiralling ever skyward.
Majestically soaring
On golden, feathered wings.
The medicinal light
Ever pulsing.
Prayers spoken
For all that life brings.

The angel's domain
Is entered on errand.
Scented and aromatic.
Fragrance filled air.
The family sleeps.
Safely protected.
Tutored in dreams with care.
Sacred eyes focused.
Holy of holies.
Earthly eyes closed,
Foetal,
Gently composed.
A child smells the air
From a soft - edged blanket.
Perfumed breeze speaks,
It says, "Mother is home".
Arms outstretched.
Faces with smiles on.
Hugs and kisses

And on the roam.
Toys and games,
Lessons for fledglings.
Slowly polished
To diamond from stone

A child's love, priceless,
Thoughtful and contented.
The parents' heart floats.
A ship at full sail.
Their world is ruled by kinship,
Knowledge, Wisdom,
Humility and courage in travail.
Loves embrace, it still has them.
Upward spiral,
In its mansions
See them run free.
They chose to be loving parents.
Their legacy always in me.

THE LOOM

As we were flown from home
Pre-existent memories Stayed,
And we,
Delivered aeronautically,
Breathe in this new facade.
We have come with multiple others
With a directive to love with ease.
The physical senses tutored.
Gently guiding the trustees.
An unquenchable
Thirst for the exquisite,
With humility as a guide,
All giving and creating,
The helping hand applied.
All are active and healthy,
Providences' kind hand prevails,
But the naked eye sees nothing,
Inner senses discern guiding trails.
Metamorphosis, the crown upon us:
The catalyst? Within truths' domain.
The challenge.
To the quill and the writer,
The positive word accepted,
Written, again and again.

Talents built through patience,
Faith offered to the light with ease,
Understanding turned to supplication,
Humbled supplicants with

Strengthened knees.
Of those who come to the ascendancy
All will courageously supply.
Choosing uplifting memories
As the summit beckons them
Still heaven high.
They teach for a golden harvest,
Give neophytes stronger limbs.
With a mantle bestowed by glory,
They fly with golden wings.
Energised and connected
We stand on stronger legs,
As gentle and flowing workers
Take the road that great love treads.
Ushering ever upwards
Firm, determined figures
Fly with a lightweight soul.
We servants are ever joy filled
As the journey
Continues to unroll.

The weavers' skill
Is tuned and perfected,
His loom honed.
And glorious tapestries spun.
The sight lifts the spirit
Of the seer
As he climbs towards the sun.
Strong with child,
Glowing, healthy and nourished,
A woman begins her courageous climb.

Love has touched her forehead,
The mystery of what is
Has been made sublime.
Her body yields to the warm comfort
Of the guide from the straights of time.
Her faith unfolds its power,
Her countenance begins to shine.
I see her smiling on the summit,
At the place of splendour upon high.
We awe at the surrounding beauty,
It draws a peaceful sigh.
The steps have born their harvest,
To those with golden wings.
In every heart is a map of promise
To where celestial joy begins.

JEWELS WITHIN CLOSED EYES

Through you are eons of wisdom
Gathered and unsealed.
You animate our hopes and ideals,
Our loves and desires are by you revealed.
And when we slumber in your arms,
That for which we long for
Is weighed within the
Softness of your breasts,
And tested in dreams
With thrills and charms.

You are the sweet pillow
That gives comfort,
You are the rock.
You are the womb that
Cradles our tender souls,
Nurturing with perception
In unison with life's wise clock.
Oh, but the fruits of
One night with you
Gives more comfort
Than a myriad of silken days
Of you bereft
One night with you
Is one that inspires our view.

You sooth our flesh
And fly with our Spirits unbound.
You are the oracle that all life seeks.
All of life knows your song
And when we are held
In your delicate wings
Mortality is but a distant kiss from
A guiding voice that speaks.
When you are in repose
Your melody of signs linger
Guiding all to their realised wishes
And where they most belong.

ELIXIR'S CHILDREN

In this time,
I look in amazement at how
Elixir has been transformed.
I see a queen amongst queens,
Glorious beyond words,
A calm, noble and sentient planet.
I marvel at her heavenly
Paradisiacal lands,
At her vibrant lakes,
Rivers and oceans teaming with life.
Her bounteous natural foods feed all.
Peaceful men and women
Grace her colourful lands;
Birds of beauty fly in her skies.
All creatures grow from her
And have become honoured by her.
Our children play with former beasts of prey,
Running freely and inhaling her
Fragrant breath.
All are happy and grateful.
Rejoicing at her mercy,
Her justice and her love.
I see men and women communing
With spirit.
Receiving sanctioned guidance and council
From Creation's higher unseen worlds.
All glory in their new wisdom.
I watched all of this,
And I smile.

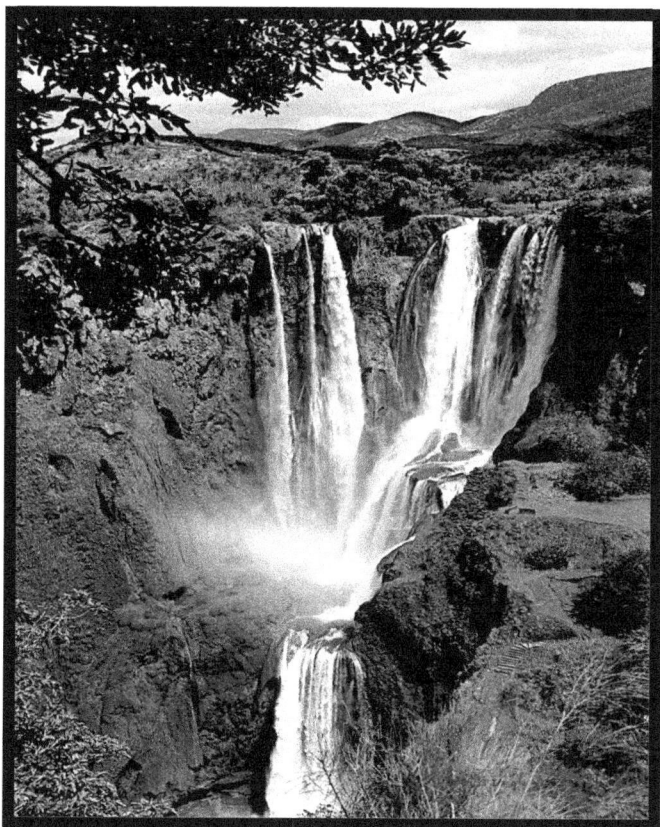

THE ELIXIAN SONG

With wings so quickly expanding,
This permeating essence it sings,
The servants' skyward thoughts reach
To gain the knowledge of sentient beings.
Minds guided and advised by the sober.
Taught within the humblest of themes.
Spoken to, made conscious and alerted,
Mentored and enabled by kind and patient beings.

Live, eat and drink in Elixir.
A reflection of what can be.
Dance, eat and drink
From our well of dreams
And golden dreams you will see.

Loves essence.
The light that frees us.
Opens our minds to be honourable beings.
To see clearly is of worthy attention
To be a free and loving being.
Communities grown, safe and healing,
Mentally freed by courageous beings.
The will to succeed and yet be humble,
The goal?
The bestowal of wealth to further enrich our beings.

Mervin Telford

Live, eat and drink in Elixir.
A reflection of what can be.
Dance, eat and drink
From our well of dreams
And golden dreams you will see.

Love causes all to realise their greatness.
They become rich with rapport.
All will have greater elation
When crowned and becoming wise beings.
We are advised to listen, to heed them,
So our work will yield great themes.
Write odes to revere and honour them.
So that in happiness we remember great beings.
To add value to life we learn
From wise and knowledgeable beings.
Life commemorates love by pairing
Loving partners merging as blissful beings.

Live, eat and drink in Elixir.
A reflection of what can be.
Dance, eat and drink
From our well of dreams
And golden dreams you will see.

Mervin Telford

FREEDOM WHISPERS

Freedom quietly whispers,

It speaks within your ears.

It says, "Every day, freedom's day

Grows stronger with the years."

We love to give surprises,

Arrayed and on display,

What sweet gifts await us?

What joys to invigorate our day?

Freedom gently whispers,

It says, "Most gifts come neatly wrapped;

They bring bravery from experience

And help us to adapt.

They build characters, make heroes,

Define us and urge to act.

Be prudent and thankful in advance

For these valuable, heartfelt joys.

Giving precious oil

From the expeller press,

Helping all towards greater poise."

THE LISTENERS' PAST

In harmony moves
A glowing crown.
Is watched with reverence,
A shimmering gown.
Through dancing crowds,
To open ear.
Gently speaking
Far and near.
All who stood and listened
No longer slept.
Held high their heads
And hearts well kept.

First breath of words,
Spoke soft to ear,
They left and loved
Both far and near.
With tempered hearts
They travelled far.
Their words guided
By an inner star.
Now wiser and older
They summarised:
The listeners' past
Had held their prize,
Embraced new love,
No longer slept.
Had found new life
And self respect.

Mervin Telford

EMBRACED

Warmth that's inviting

Our summer is gold,

Love is released

From friendships threshold.

A benevolent presence

Invisible but felt.

Our faith has flourished

Where empathy is spelt.

Comfort is magnified

Made bountiful at home,

By diligent ears,

Hearing a beautiful tone.

Attracted by a sweetened heart,

By a mind that sent love.

Guided thoughts,

Attentive to trust

Within a clean head start.

Our hearts glow, shining,

Where angels now dance.

The present is exciting,

Loves' listeners entranced.

Sanctity approaches,

Deployed by the positive tongue.

Blessed to be grateful.

Our destiny is spun.

Reborn strength

The living waters acquire.

Volcanic vortex'

Swirling axis,

Rising higher and higher.

As lovers we have awakened,

Truths sacred escorts.

Joyous sweet visions,

Embraced,

Beautiful thoughts.

LOVE MANTRA

Love can be seen

Your eyes are refined.

Love can be heard,

Its emotion has sound.

Love can be smelled,

Its fragrance abounds.

Love can be felt,

Soothing hearts all around.

Mervin Telford

A HEALER CALLED JOY

Velvet green meadows,
Undulate and bask.
Lovingly stroked
Through nimbus clouds
By soft silver fingers
Of an adoring sun.
Seasonal jewels
Hang, shine and sway;
The fruit of our limbs
Enticing your senses
In this warm, easy breeze.

We dine on
Sweet nutrient,
Succulent
Within Molasses soil,
Malleable yet firm.
With instrumental elements
We compose harmonics
That speaks to super nature.
Our remedial symphonies
Radiate indiscernibly
From your live,
Green themed paintings.

Opals of transparent silver
Travel to and fro.
Their occupants unaware of the
Iridescent auroras
And shining subtle vortexes.
Synchronised and invisible,
Landscapes within landscapes.
We channel harmonic frequencies,
Their essences permeate
With atomic particles that rise,
Glide, re-configure,
Onward sail and reform.

My family reach skyward,
Globally rooted,
Yet growing to the sun.
Prayerfully we invoke
Warmth and balance into the
Inner domains of the beloved.
The heavens respond
And gems are born from seeds.
We as ancient conduits
Are your silent healers,
And I am a healer called Joy.

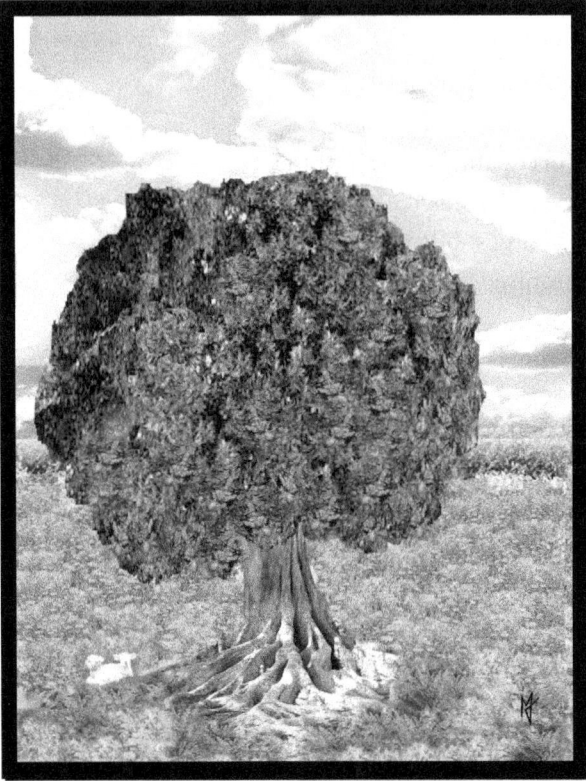

Mervin Telford

THE SHELLS OF ELIXIR

To create with love! An enduring gift.
Causality! To every action a beautiful consequence!

Prisms of light sparkle and flicker through
Plumes of volumous clouds.
Within their striated beams seedlings spark into life.
They glitter and swirl, mixing with winds and heavy
rainfall.
Powerful gusts choreograph the swaying foliage,
Dancing and leaping in the colour filled landscape
beneath.

Pebble sized seedlings impact the ground upon contact,
Burrowing into the soft, rich soil.
Suddenly! From the stillness of the rainstorm's release,
Countless wings explode, bursting from the green trees'
canopies.
Their flurry of feathers filling the moist air
With the sound of muted flapping.
Clouds of paradisiacal birds move in formation.
Colours of the rainbow that are etched within their
feathers,
Create electrifying displays as they swirl and twist,
Maneuvering to observe the strange new
Movements occurring in the landscape below.
Tiny mounds push upwards out of the soil, expanding
And rising through the lush vegetation.
Matt white, translucent structures.
Opaque, spiraled and fast growing

Fasten themselves like magnificent giant shells.
Rooted and contrasting, yet complimenting
The lush, rich colour speckled landscape.

We have never fathomed how these shells came to be.
We were amazed when at first contact the shells
opened.
Through a flexible yet firm membrane the first of us
experienced
The inner domain of the shells.
It was then that we Elixians amazingly
Discovered our new, live homes.
The shells produced a subtle usable power
And channeled the day light into all its chambers.
Perfectly circulating the "I am all" energy.
Inside them our senses where enhanced.
Our thought processes became
More efficient and we grew to be ever more intuitive.
Our bodies have also become stronger
And healthier from the purifying atmosphere within.
Life spans are magnified.
Increased vitality is had by all.
The prisms of light delivered more seeds as
Families grew and we flourished.
Paradise is now ever expanding.
Our abilities have increased
And we have become known as the seers of Elixir.

Mervin Telford

TO AIDN I CAME

To Aidn I came.
Today I saw things
That will always allow me to
Appreciate service and love.

I saw volunteers,
Healers of men standing
Feet to knees emerged
By light filled liquid,
Further enriching
Beautiful garments.
With Fragrant,
Perfumed essences.
Delivered by skilled,
Caring hands,
Gently caressing and purifying cloaks
With smooth, moist ether of alabaster.
Over and over.
Glowing and love infused.
Ready for the wearer.
Hour after hour,
Day after day,
Re-igniting,
Re-defining
Re-energising.

To Aidn I came.
Today I saw things
That will always allow me to
Appreciate service and love.

Mervin Telford

I saw gifted children
Realise their talents and inner wealth.
Tiny hands
Raised in thanksgiving and praise.
A playful nudge and pull at a sleeve.
A teacher's tender advice.

Confident,
Asking,
Requesting an assignment.
Smiling thereafter. Understanding and patient.
An Elixian seer walks amongst us.
His shimmering garments
Slowly Swissshhh against the marble floor
His crystal-like eyes look skyward,
As if in silent prayer,
"I am all, THAT I am, I am all, THAT I am,"
Is chanted by his soft, strong voice,
A voice made audible
By a reverent silence.
All smile inwardly
At the familiarity and meaning
Of his words.

Divinity moves gracefully
Weaving through the crowd.
I look again closely,
I see strong, supple peoples,
Powerfully jointed,
Reinforced:
This is the Devine in
Man, Woman and child.
Remade and reformed.
They walk on higher
Levels of being,
Giving as they do so.
Continually they pass
Each other,

Mervin Telford

Each into his own eyes.
There they see the Devine.
Long ago infused,
Sensitised by those
With stronger limbs
The seers of old,
The healed ones
Who re-invented
The children of the fruitful,
With healing hearts as gifts.
Their emblem of revival.

To Aidn I came.
Today I saw things
That will always allow me to
Appreciate service and love.

THE PATH

We walk this plane with humble attire,
The harmonic path has re-addressed.
For Love is nurture, reality forming
New perspectives in warmth caressed.
We use the keys and test our strength
With visualisation in silence's length.

We expand the light that shines so bright.
In silent communion we control the sight.
Merging grids of energy sharing.
Love is conducting, empaths pairing
Mass thought cohesive grown in time.
The created image, planet sublime.

Speak with power and turn the key,
Use the word and you will see.
Emerging with faith, knowledge
And a healing hand.
Souls migrate to the Promised Land.

Mervin Telford

FOR YOU

What do I do for you?
I grow food for you,
Ask the skies to rain for you,
The sun to shine for you,
Constellations to form for you,
Bring you bounteous forests,
Fields and orchards to nourish you,
Create oceans with life for you,
Fly the dimensional planes with you,
Build bridges for us to cross to the
Gardens I create to dance free with you.
I made these havens for us to be
Loving together incredibly
For eternity.
This I do for you,
Now fly free.

Mervin Telford

THE HEALING

Moved by the power of your heartfelt prayer
We left our homes and journeyed here
We chose to come and help repair
And gently heal you.

Through elements we flew and marched
To find many of you wishful,
Lost and parched.
We have come to gently heal you.

Over ecru deserts', mountains' seas'.
Your prayers have succeeded
Now hear our pleas.
Will you help us to gently heal you?

Dry your tears and help us know.
Make strong again your colourful wings.
Clean the soil from your delicate brow
And together we will gently heal you.

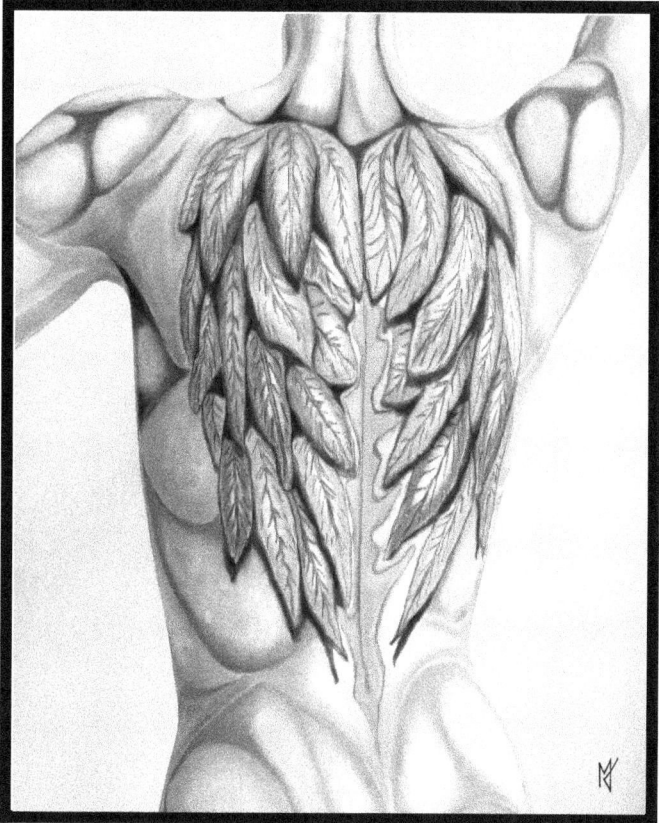

Mervin Telford

A MESSAGE TO YOU

My spirit hears of ancient tales of kinship,
Salutations amongst the victorious and
Shouts of joy after liberation. I see the
Warmth of camaraderie that radiates from
A brave, noble face and a strength that
Emanates from the windows of your loving eyes.

The Master artists' brush has with patience
And care adorned your canvas. When you are
Truly aware of this your spirit will sing with
Joy and you will be held in an exquisite
Spectrum, a moving colour filled symphony
Created within the vortex of your soul.
Your highest dreams and ideals will be
Manifested as the holograms illusion changes
To tender in the presence of who you really are.
My spirit looks on in awe, perceiving the
Metamorphosis that lays ahead.

Great crafters shape their jewels with both
Assertive wisdom and tenderness so has it has
Been with you. Shaped by determined intent
And gentleness of hand and imbued with love. You
Are gifted with distinctive qualities that
Provides you with the requisite tools needed to
Complete the unique tasks that lay before you
Beckoning you onwards. Embrace these qualities,
For you are to humanity as a jewel is to a crown.

You are to be told at this time that it is you
Who chooses who it is that you wish to
Become. Your potential is unlimited and
Largely governed by your perception of what
Is achievable. Awareness of the imagery you
Allow into your mind is paramount for
"As one thinks so one is". As you continue
To harness energy and strength through
Positive endeavours you will become more
Aware of the sanctity and beauty of your body,
Mind, spirit and your connection to all who
Move within life's grand tapestry. Ultimately
The choices to be made are yours. Free
Agency will always be respected, regardless
Of the paths that are traversed. You will
Always be loved.

As you may know you have had and always
Will have help with you at all times, even
When you sleep. Be aware, the spoken word
Has power, use it wisely. You need only to
Ask in humility and faith and all that you
Need shall be provided for in the fullness of
Time. Know that you are loved and cherished,
And have been nurtured from your earliest
Inception. Also know that all that has
Happened has been for your benefit and
Wisdom. There are lessons being taught both
By you and to you at every encounter and
Every turn along your life's path. Be
Conscious of the hidden codes that lay within

These encounters, they are most beneficial to
Your growth and unfolding awareness.

Know that you are much loved and blessed in
These tremendous times and that a future
Awaits you that is beautiful beyond
Description. May strength and honour be
Yours for the good that you do in your
Present realm of existence and remember
The things we do in this life echo through eternity.

Thru and from this ink
To you, a very special representative of the most high.
Peace and love.

Yours friend and brother,

Mervin Telford

www.ingramcontent.com/pod-product-compliance
Lightning Source LLC
Chambersburg PA
CBHW061735020426
42331CB00006B/1245